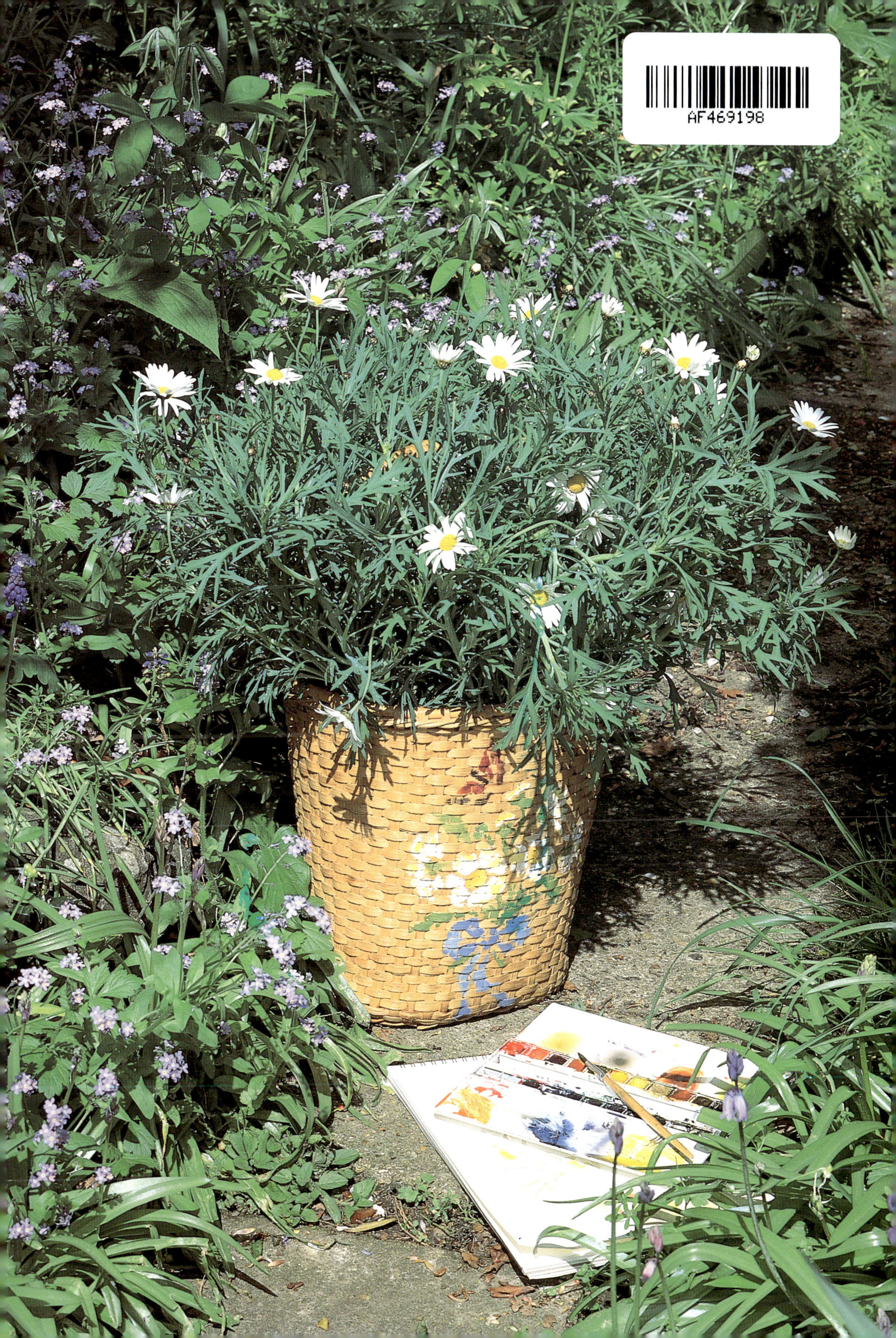
AF469198

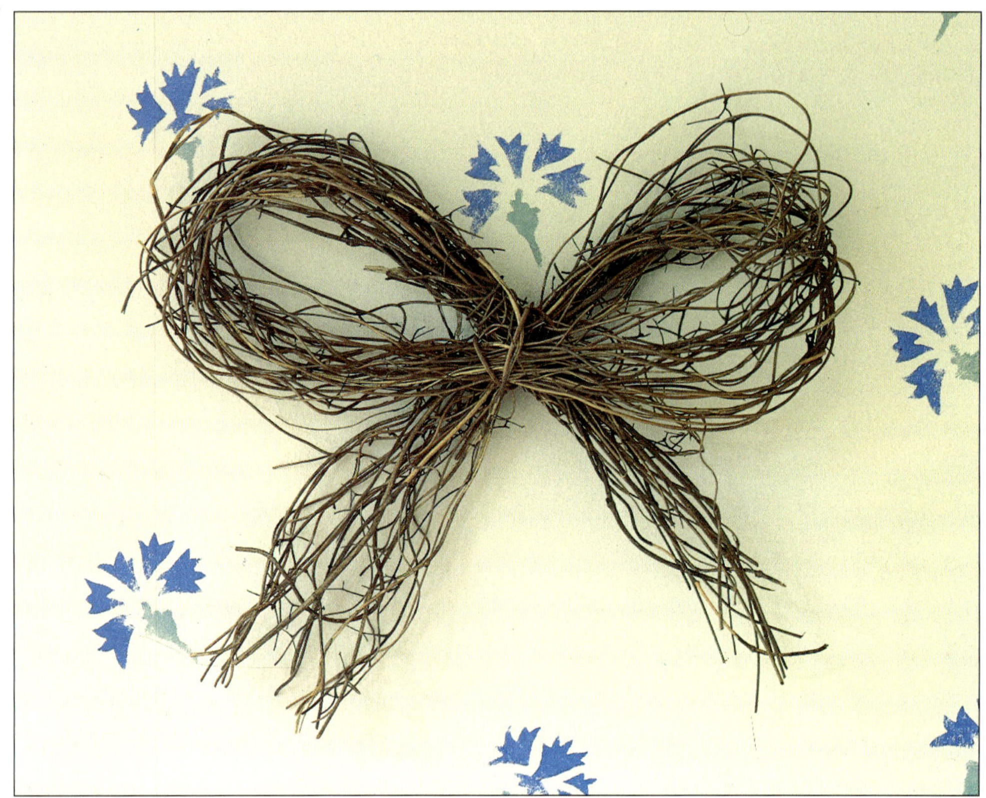

THE SPARKLE OF SUMMER, INDOORS AND OUT

You don't need green fingers to grow your own wild garden, in an instant. You need a soft brush, a few paint colours, and one of the fresh and charming designs from the 'Painted Meadow' stencil collection. Nothing looks prettier, or cooler, on a scorching day, than the breezy contrast of white and blue, like foam edged breakers, a summer sky, or the crisp simplicity of these cornflower and daisy stencils. Like all our sets of stencils this one has endless decorative possibilities, indoors and out. Use a motif to smarten up the cheapest planter, or scatter a single cornflower motif over plain painted walls to create the most exclusive 'wallpaper' around.

It takes less than no time to give your home extra flower-power, following our detailed step-by-step pictures and instructions, which are designed to make the process a doddle even if you have never picked up a brush before. And it's fun seeing flowers spring up in an instant, knowing that with a lick or two of varnish, they could last a lifetime.

As well as giving technical tips for professional results, these stencil books are packed with fresh and inventive ideas for adding impact and personality to all sorts of surfaces around your home – from walls to floors, furniture to fabrics. Using the same designs on many of the components of a room is a smart way of creating visual harmony, as the pictures in this book reveal.

The stencils are pre-cut from heavy-duty melamine, flexible enough to bend round corners, transparent for easy registration, and just about indestructible. On the following pages we show you how to combine colours and shades, and how to use stencil elements in different ways and to fit tricky situations.

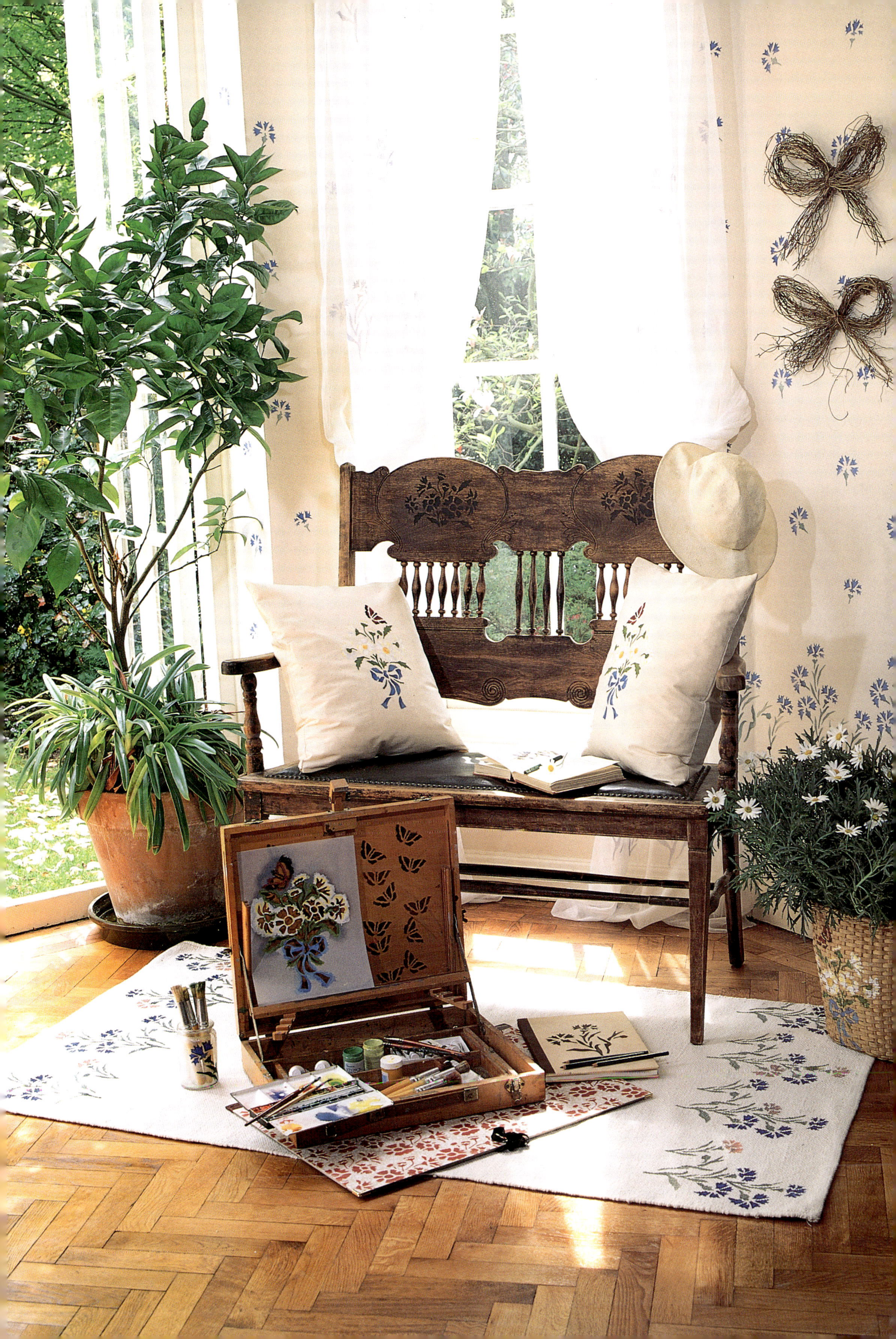

Stencilling know-how starts here

Nowadays most professional stencillers choose soft, bushy brushes, like the ones below, applying colour very sparingly with a round-and-round motion to create soft, clear 'prints'. Beginners always use too much paint and a wet brush, which makes splats, and paint tends to creep under the stencil edges. So after picking up colour on your brush, rub it on newspaper to force colour up the bristles and blot surplus moisture. This is the whole secret of crisp, airy stencils. The paint you choose is less important – artists' acrylics, specialist stencil colours, even odds and ends of household emulsions all work well.

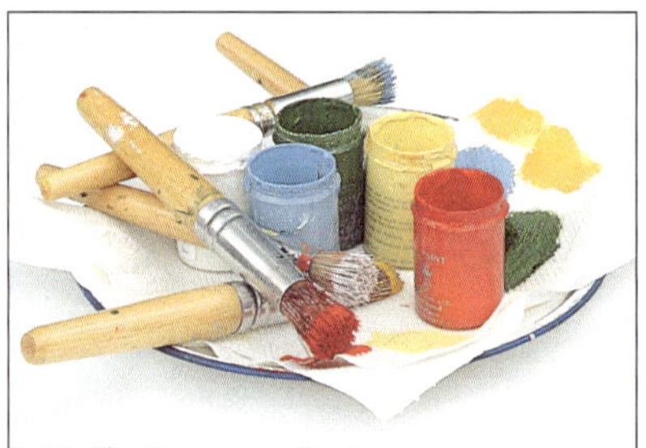

There's no need for an expensive range of paint colours either. The wild flowers featured in our 'Painted Meadow' series are deliciously simple both in colour and shape, and your stencilling should respect that natural freshness. A set of basic colours, as shown on the left, should be enough if you mix them (like yellow and blue for green) to create more shades. Buy two or three brushes in different sizes – large, medium and small, plus one pointed watercolour brush for fine detail.

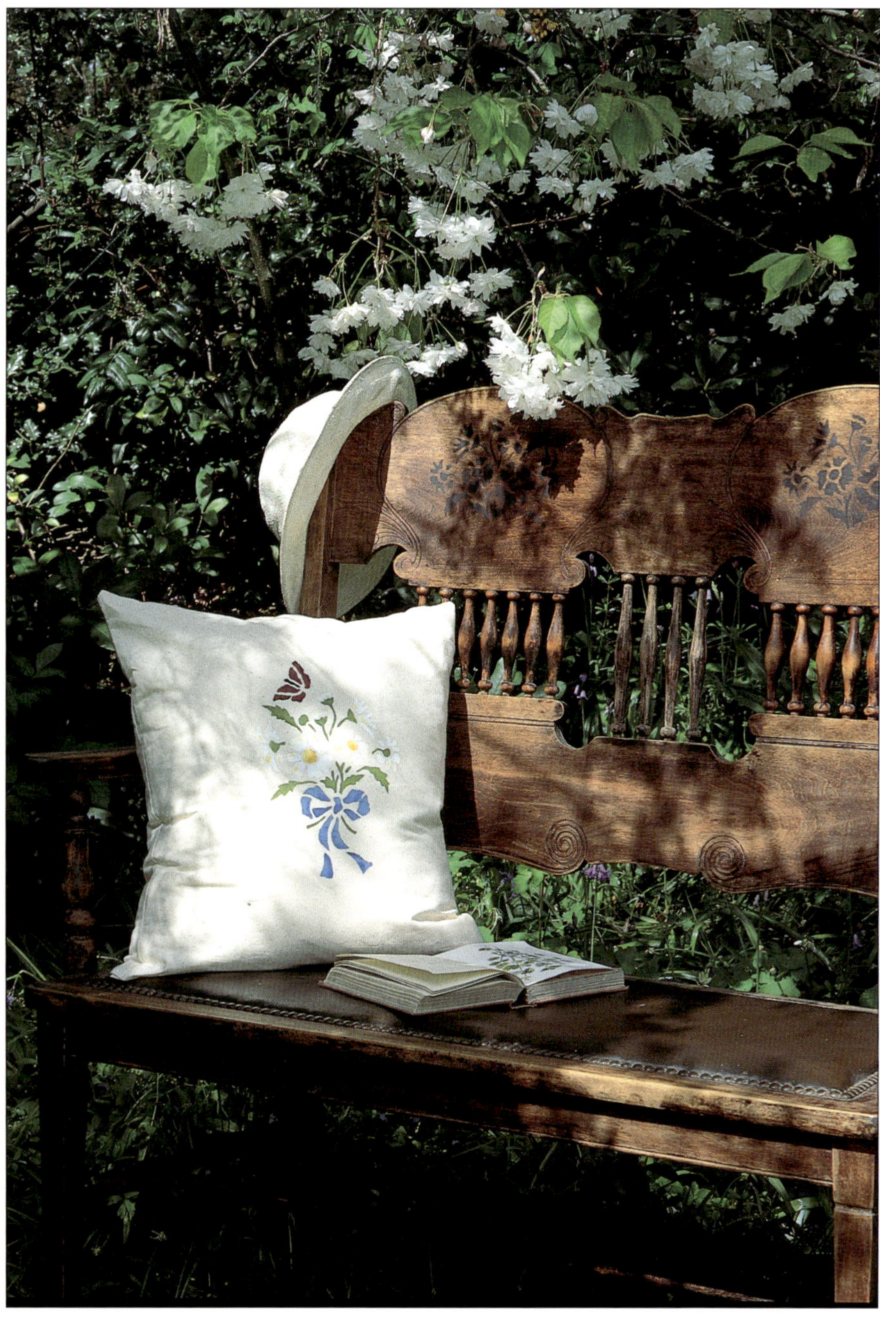

The big picture on the previous page shows our stencils used over a wide range of surfaces; decorating the wall, highlighting cushions, notebooks and folders, and bordering a pretty floorcloth. Without looking contrived, the overall effect is as refreshing as a milk shake.

Below, on a stencilled bench, a silk cushion cover sports a be-ribboned posy of daisies and cornflowers. Specialist fabric paints were used to create a washable fabric decoration with all the elegance of something hand-painted and unique.

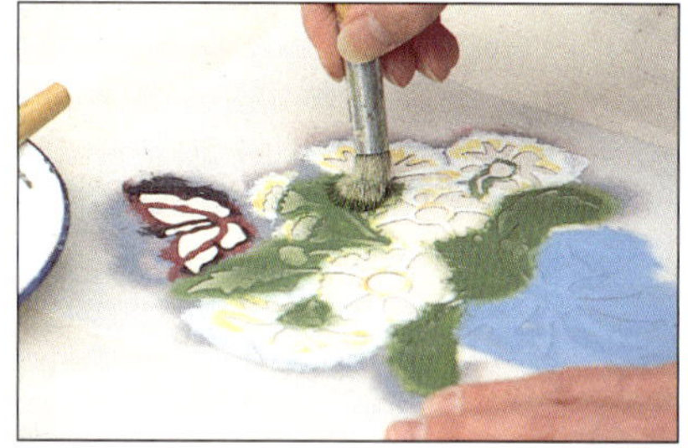

To create a four-colour posy, start by taping the stencil firmly to some grey silk cushion cover fabric. Then brush in the green leaves, followed by the white daisies.

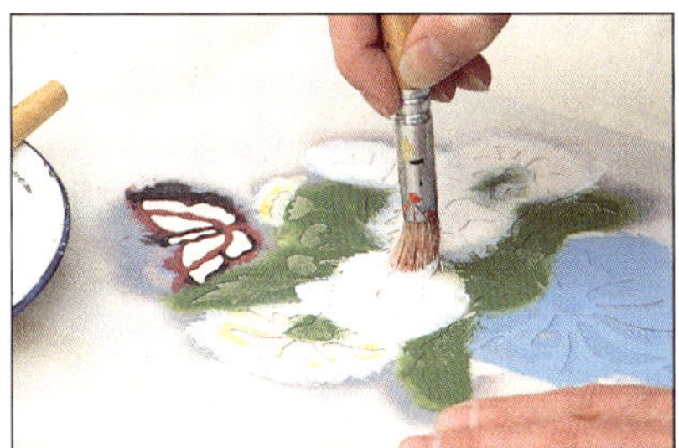

A dot of golden yellow gives the daisies their striking and joyful hearts. Use a smaller brush for this free-hand touch.

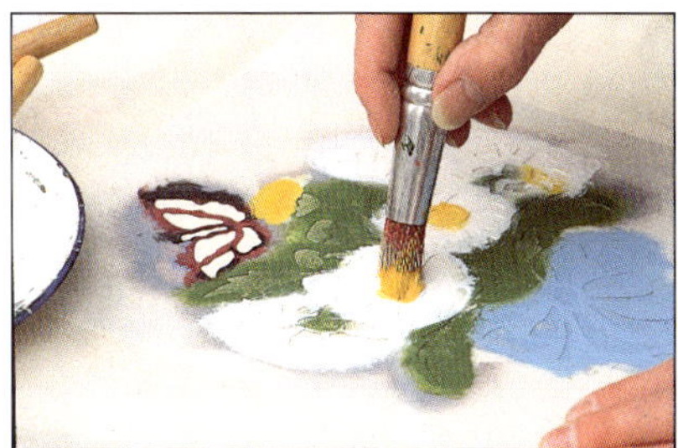

Red butterflies may be rare in nature but a touch of red brings our composition to life, and is balanced by the blue bow beneath.

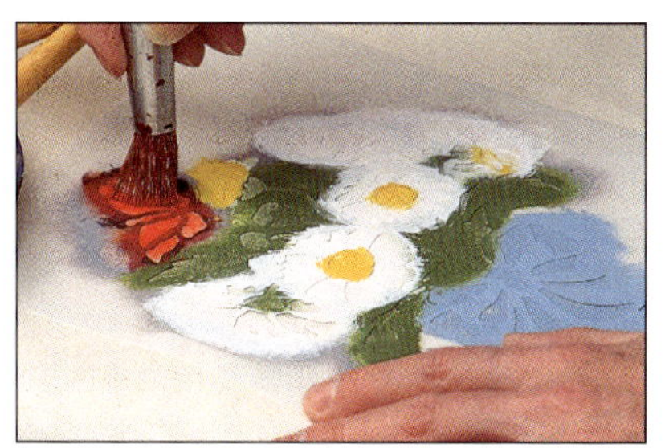

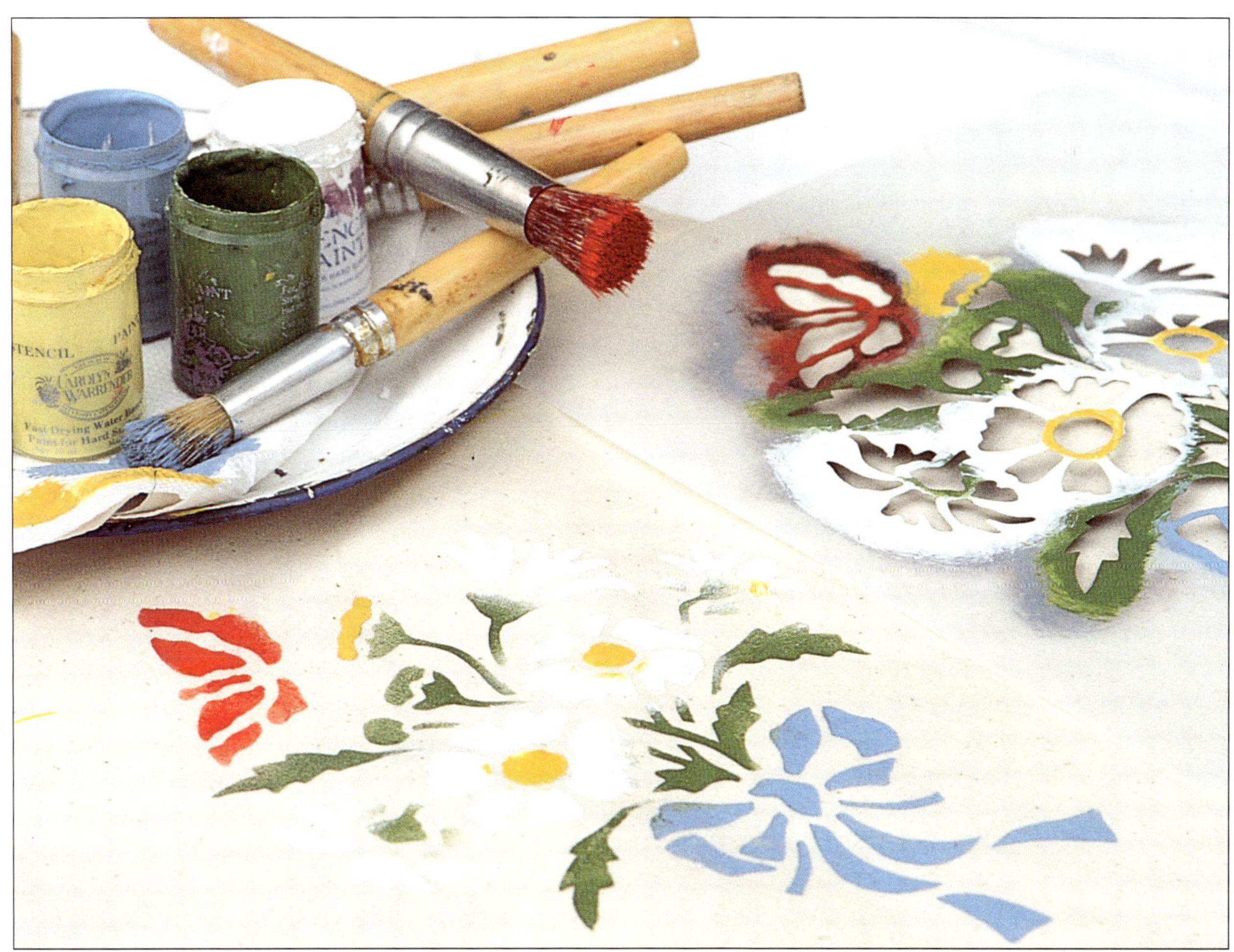

Once the fabric paints are dry, you will need to fix them with a warm iron, according to the manufacturer's instructions. You should also refer to these instructions for advice on washing the finished cushion cover.

When stencilling on an uneven surface, like our basket planter, it is sensible to tape the stencil down with pieces of masking tape to stop it moving about as you paint. The design here has been 'whited out', prior to applying final colours, in order to make the pale shades stand out clearly against the brown background. This is usual practice when stencilling in pale colours on a darker ground. Use white acrylic, which dries instantly.

The next stage is to go over the white stencil, using green for the leaves, blue for the bow and yellow for the daisy centres. It is sensible to protect an item like this with clear matt varnish.

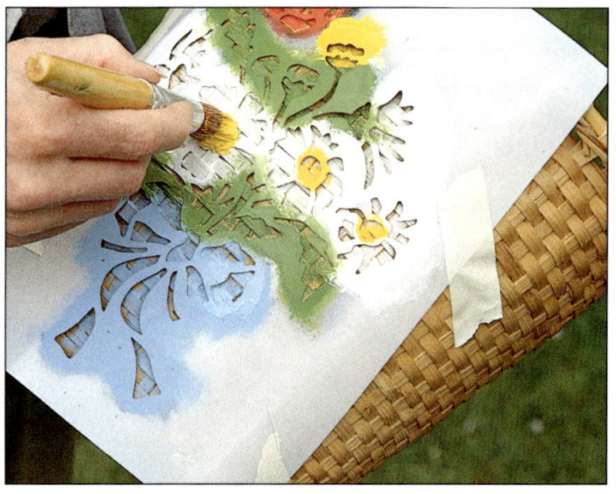

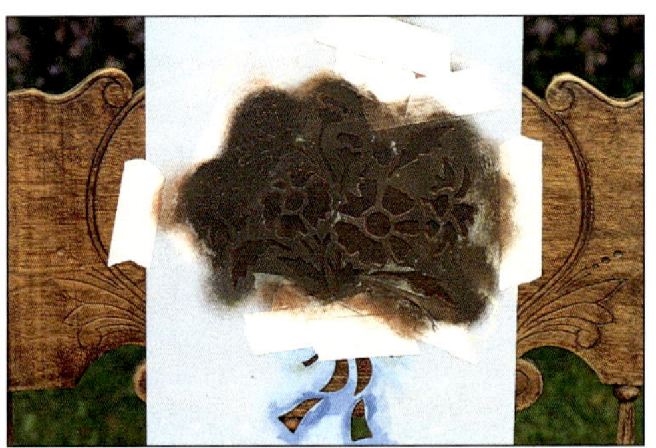

A completely different and sophisticated effect can be obtained by using the same designs in 'unnatural' colours. The motif used on this attractive wooden seat has been stencilled in brownish-black, to produce a marquetry effect in keeping with its Art Nouveau curves. Again the stencil should be varnished for protection.

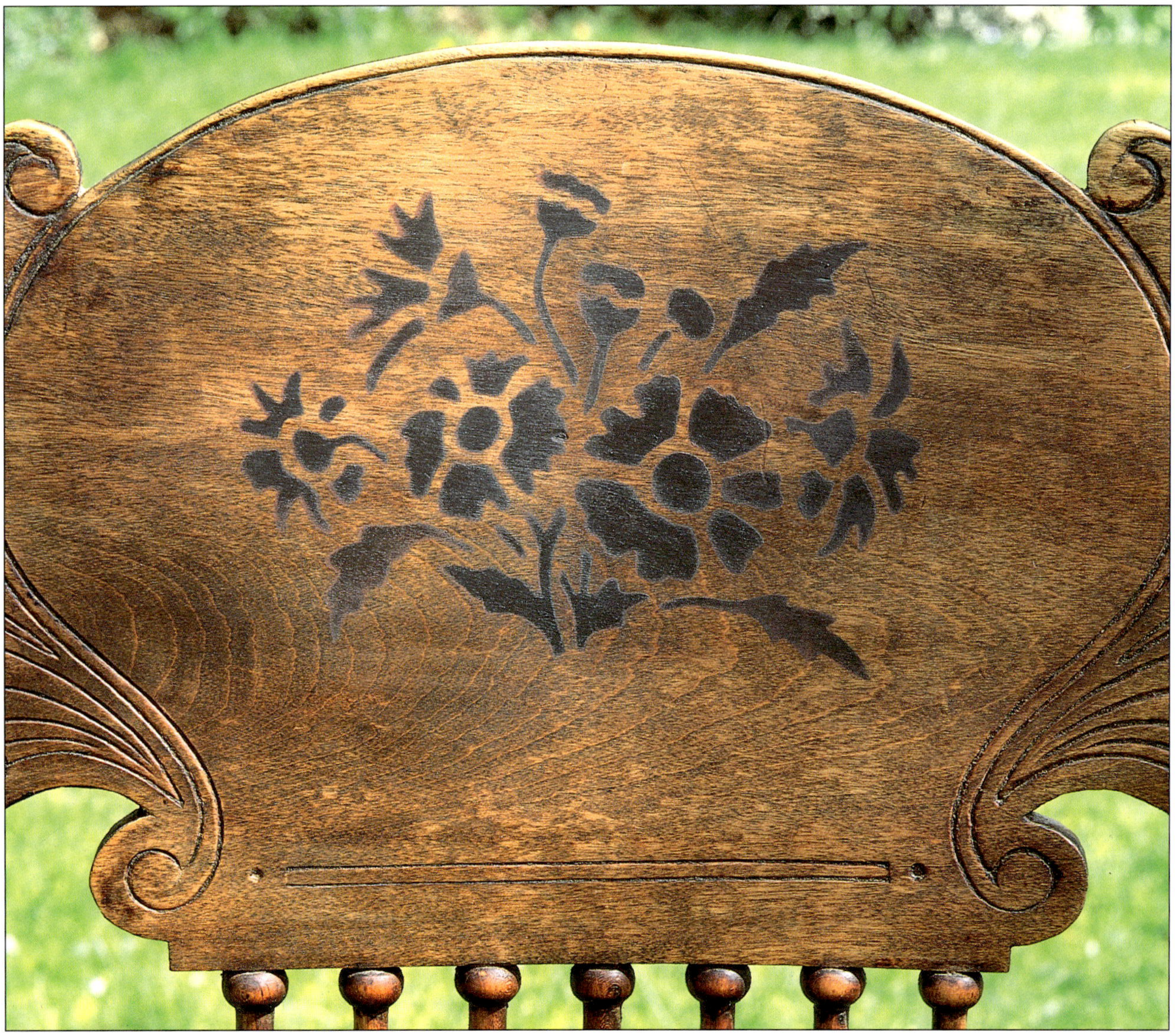

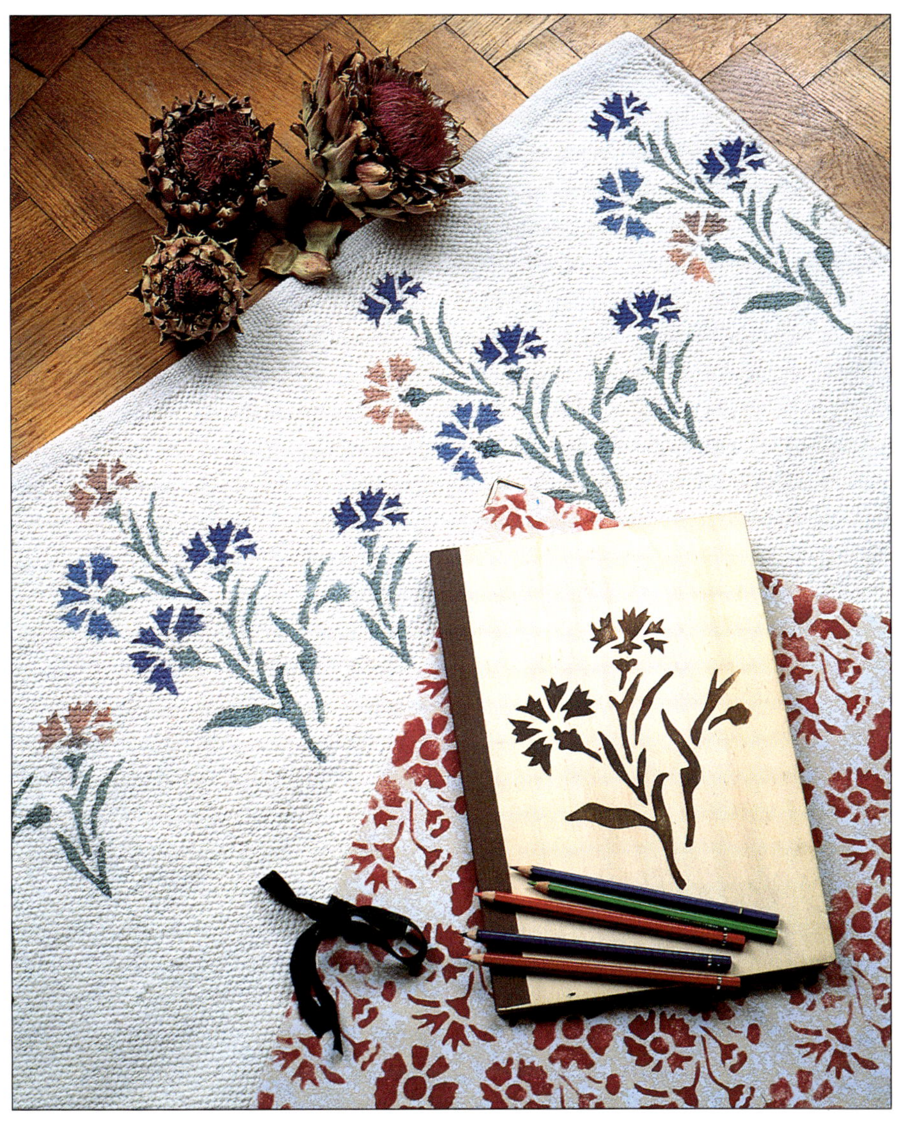

Don't be afraid to use some artistic licence if it makes for stylish decoration. Notice here how the blue cornflowers bordering a pale rug have been perked up by an occasional red interloper, and how the daisy and cornflower have both been used to create a design in red on this folder. Designs like this take a little more time, but look irresistible, and give the homeliest object an instant look of luxury.

Stencil a simple border by sliding the motif along, as shown. A small single flower softens the break between motifs. Use a touch of green, lightly stippled, on the cornflower, and a touch of blue on the leaves. This makes the stencils 'lie down'.

Stencilling on soft muslin drapes is always done using a specialist fabric paint. Lay a large sheet of soft paper behind the fabric, to mop up any surplus colour and keep the work immaculate. Stencils look wonderful on sheer fabrics, like embroidery or lace.

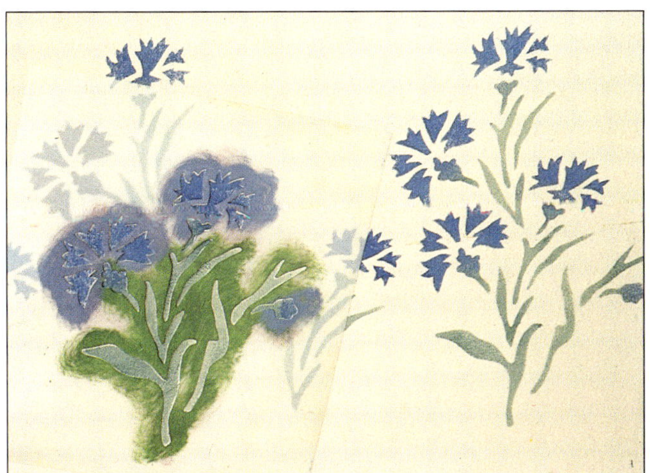

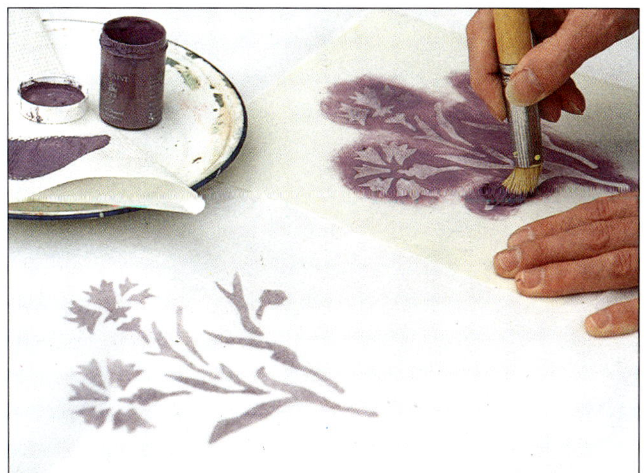

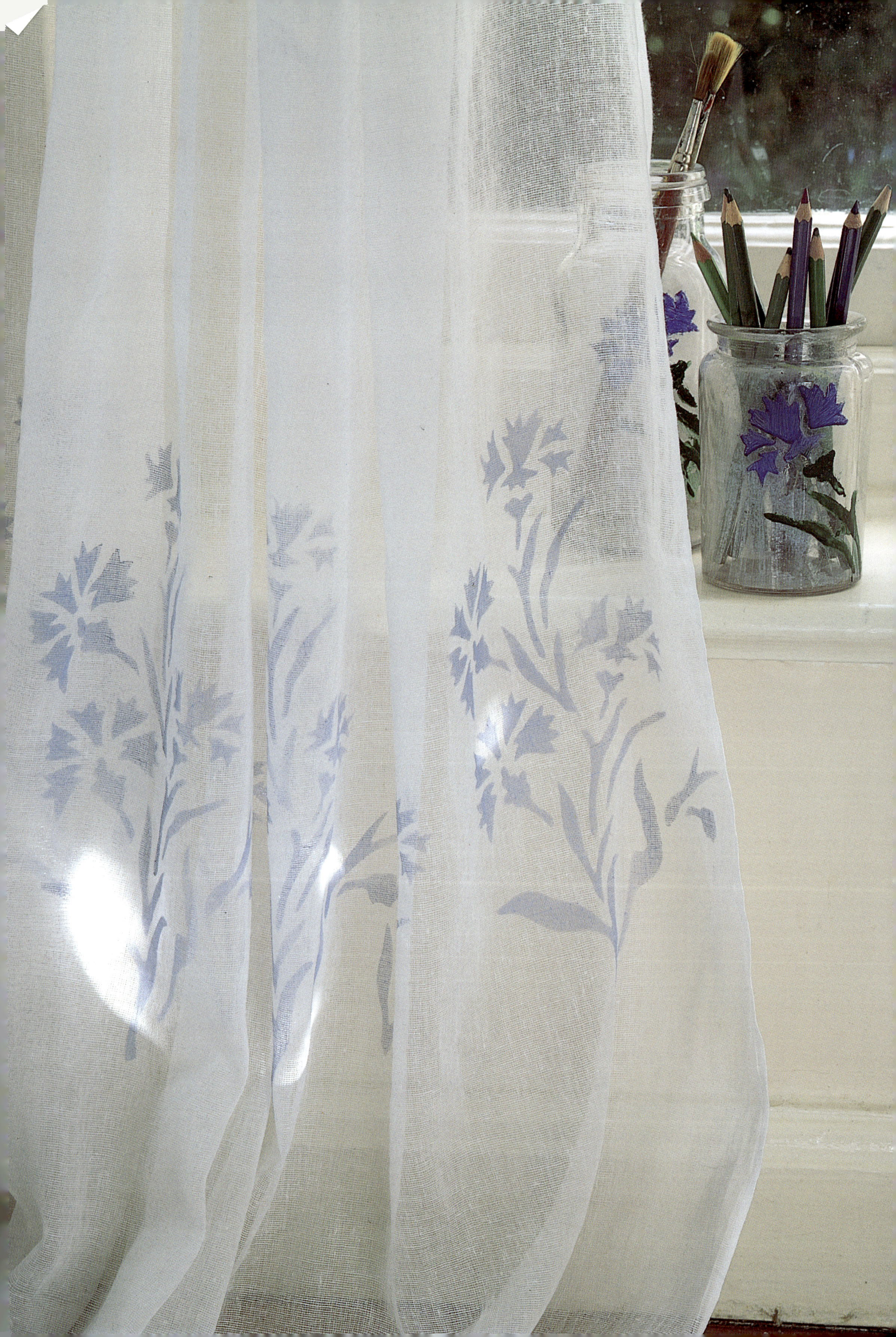